Storms

By Sophia Evans

Library For All Ltd.

Library For All is an Australian not for profit organisation with a mission to make knowledge accessible to all via an innovative digital library solution.
Visit us at libraryforall.org

Storms

First published 2021

Published by Library For All Ltd
Email: info@libraryforall.org
URL: libraryforall.org

This work is licensed under the Creative Commons Attribution-NonCommercial-NoDerivatives 4.0 International License. To view a copy of this license, visit http://creativecommons.org/licenses/by-nc-nd/4.0/.

This book was made possible by the generous support of the Education Cooperation Program and the following organisations.

  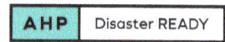

Storms
Evans, Sophia
ISBN: 978-1-922550-23-1
SKU01573

Images sourced from pixabay.com, and commons.wikimedia.org under a CCO license.

Storms

Weather

Every day the Earth's surface is bombarded with a variety of weather events. Weather is the temperature, rainfall, sunshine, cloudiness, humidity and air pressure in an area at any point in time.

Did you know?

Extreme weather events can have global impacts.

Each day, there might be a different type of weather. This weather affects the activities we do and the clothes we wear; it can even impact where we choose to live.

Storms

A storm is one example of extreme weather. During a storm, strong winds, heavy rain, hail, thunder and lightning occur; sometimes all at the same time!

Storms can last a long time or a short time. It is important to keep yourself and your family safe during a storm.

Storms near the coast can produce devastating destruction due to the violent winds whipping up coastal waters, as well as furious rain and hail.

The enormous forces created by storms can destroy houses, forests and even whole cities. Even if you live nowhere near the coast, storms can have devastating effects.

Rain and hail

Rain and hail are both formed inside clouds before falling to the Earth. When moisture evaporates from the ground it rises, causing an updraft that combines water and ice particles.

The particles start out smaller than a grain of sand, and grow as they join other particles within the cloud.

Once there are enough particles sticking together, they are too heavy and fall to the ground as rain or hail.

A single rain cloud can hold enough water to fill a swimming pool!

Lightning

Sometimes when particles of water and ice collide in clouds, they create a form of static electricity. Lightning is this electricity that jumps between clouds and the ground. A nearby lightning strike may make a loud 'crack' when it hits due to the amount of energy discharged.

While small static electricity charges may give you a bit of a jolt; a hit from lightning holds enough built-up energy to kill a person. It is important to remain indoors when there is lightning so that you don't get hurt.

Thunder

Thunder happens at the same time as lightning even though it doesn't seem so. This is because light travels faster than sound so we see the lightning bolt first.

Usually you will hear the clouds rumbling before a storm. This is because the static electricity is building up in the clouds forming lightning, thunder, rain and hail.

Wind

When air is moving it is called wind. Some winds are slow and help you cool down on a hot day. Some winds are fast and can cause widespread damage. Strong winds create flying debris made of branches or dirt.

Ocean winds can create devastating ocean waves.

Did you know?

Winds cause damage by knocking over trees, power lines and even blowing roofs off houses. Winds travel fast over the ocean because there is nothing in the way to slow them down.

Know the signs

Before a storm there are many signs to look for.

1. Clouds get darker because they are full of rain.

2. The sound of thunder rumbling can be heard as a storm gets closer.

3. The wind can get stronger and you can see branches moving or dirt flying.

4 The wind can sometimes change direction or whip around.

5 You might be able to smell rain as moisture fills the air.

6 Ocean waves might get bigger or choppier, boats get very bumpy in stormy weather.

7 Rain might start to fall slowly or quickly.

Did you know?

Storms can happen at any time and can seem to come out of nowhere. It is important to be prepared before a storm hits so that you, your family and animals are safe.

Be prepared

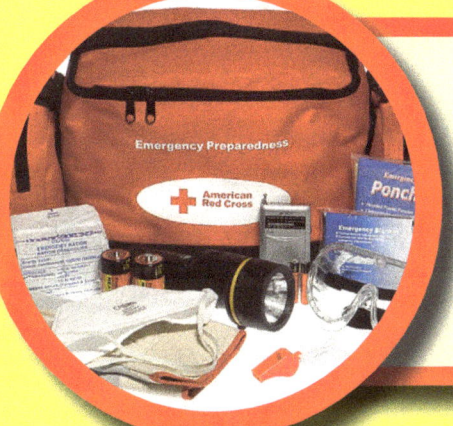

An emergency kit is a kit your family has put together that includes at least 3 days' supplies in case your village or house becomes isolated.

A safety plan is what your family decides to do if there is an emergency. Having a safety plan is essential so that everyone knows what to do and where to go. Your community can give your family advice on the best plan for your area.

It is a good idea to have an emergency kit and a safety plan just in case a storm happens. Each person has a different job to do to get prepared.

Emergency kit

No matter where you live or what the weather is like: it is vital that every house has an emergency kit. An emergency kit is stored in a sturdy, waterproof container and includes lots of items to keep you healthy, safe and informed.

A good emergency kit includes:
- A first aid kit (with any medication you need);
- Tinned food and a can opener;
- Waterproof matches and a way to cook your food;
- Bottled water;
- Warm, dry clothes;
- Battery operated radio and batteries;
- And toiletries (including toilet paper, toothpaste, insect repellent and a mosquito net.)

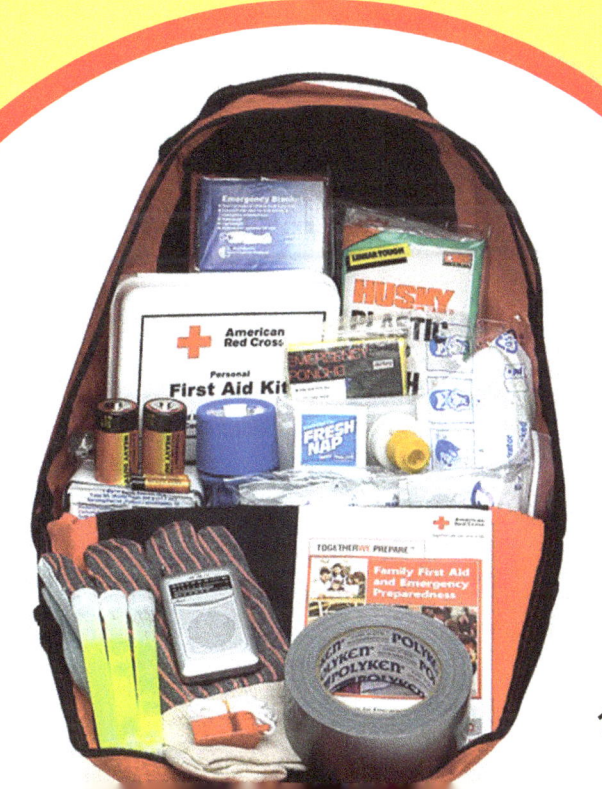

Stay safe

1

Stay inside until the storm has stopped.

2

Stay out of flood water; there could be dangers beneath the surface.

3

Stay away from windows in case of hail or flying debris.

4

Stay away from trees as they could fall over or they could be hit by lightning.

5 Stay up to date. Use a radio to hear any important information or announcements.

6

Stay in contact with your neighbours so they are safe too.

7 Stay away from fallen power lines or electrical equipment. They could be dangerous.

It's time to prepare for an emergency!

Use your finger to trace the lines. Which items should go into the emergency kit? Which ones should stay at home?

Photo credits

Page	Link
Cover	https://commons.wikimedia.org/wiki/File:Manila_Philippines_Tropical-storm-over-Pasig-River-01.jpg
Title Cover	https://pixabay.com/photos/lightning-thunder-lightning-storm-1056419/
4-5	https://pixabay.com/photos/dawn-sun-mountain-landscape-sky-190055/
6-7	https://pixabay.com/photos/lightning-thunder-lightning-storm-1056419/ https://pixabay.com/photos/hurricane-devastation-destruction-2019494/ https://pixabay.com/photos/key-west-florida-hurricane-dennis-81665/
9	https://pixabay.com/photos/cumulonimbus-storm-hunting-3196780/
10-11	https://pixabay.com/photos/lightning-thunder-lightning-storm-1056419/ https://pixabay.com/photos/lightning-thunder-thunderstorm-1845/ https://it.wikipedia.org/wiki/File:LightningOverMiramareDiRiminiItaly.jpg
12-13	https://pixabay.com/photos/lightning-thunder-lightning-storm-1056419/
14-15	https://pixabay.com/photos/hurricane-devastation-destruction-2019494/ https://commons.wikimedia.org/wiki/File:Katrina-port-sulphur-la-2005.jpg
18-19	https://pixabay.com/photos/key-west-florida-hurricane-dennis-81664/ https://commons.wikimedia.org/wiki/File:FEMA_-_37174_-_Emergency_Preparedness_%22ready_to_go%22_kit..jpg
20-21	https://commons.wikimedia.org/wiki/File:FEMA_-_40042_-_Student_smiles_with_her_student_%22starter%22_emergency_kit.jpg https://commons.wikimedia.org/wiki/File:Be_Prepared,_All_Year_Long_160928-F-DD155-0015.jpg https://commons.wikimedia.org/wiki/File:FEMA_-_37173_-_Red_Cross_%22ready_to_go%22_preparedness_kit.jpg
22-23	https://pixabay.com/photos/person-little-boy-kid-child-731165/ http://turbulens.net/wp-content/uploads/Pixabay_Flood_Uknownplace.jpg https://pixabay.com/photos/hail-storm-thunderstorm-forest-123042/ https://pixabay.com/photos/radio-vintage-retro-music-old-821602/ https://commons.wikimedia.org/wiki/File:US_Navy_100505-N-5862D-017_Chief_Petty_Officer_Jason_Reynolds_helps_his_neighbors_pack_their_household_goods_into_a_storage_trailer_at_Naval_Support_Activity_Mid-South_in_Millington,_Tenn.jpg https://commons.wikimedia.org/wiki/File:Cyclone_Marcus_in_Darwin_%E2%80%93_Fallen_power_lines_and_pole_02.jpg

Emergency decision-making tree

Prior to the event of a tsunami, tropical cyclone, flooding, landslide or earthquake, speak with your family and teacher about your community's evacuation building or safe place.

Discuss how to respond to possible scenarios, and use the decision tree to help you decide the best course of action.

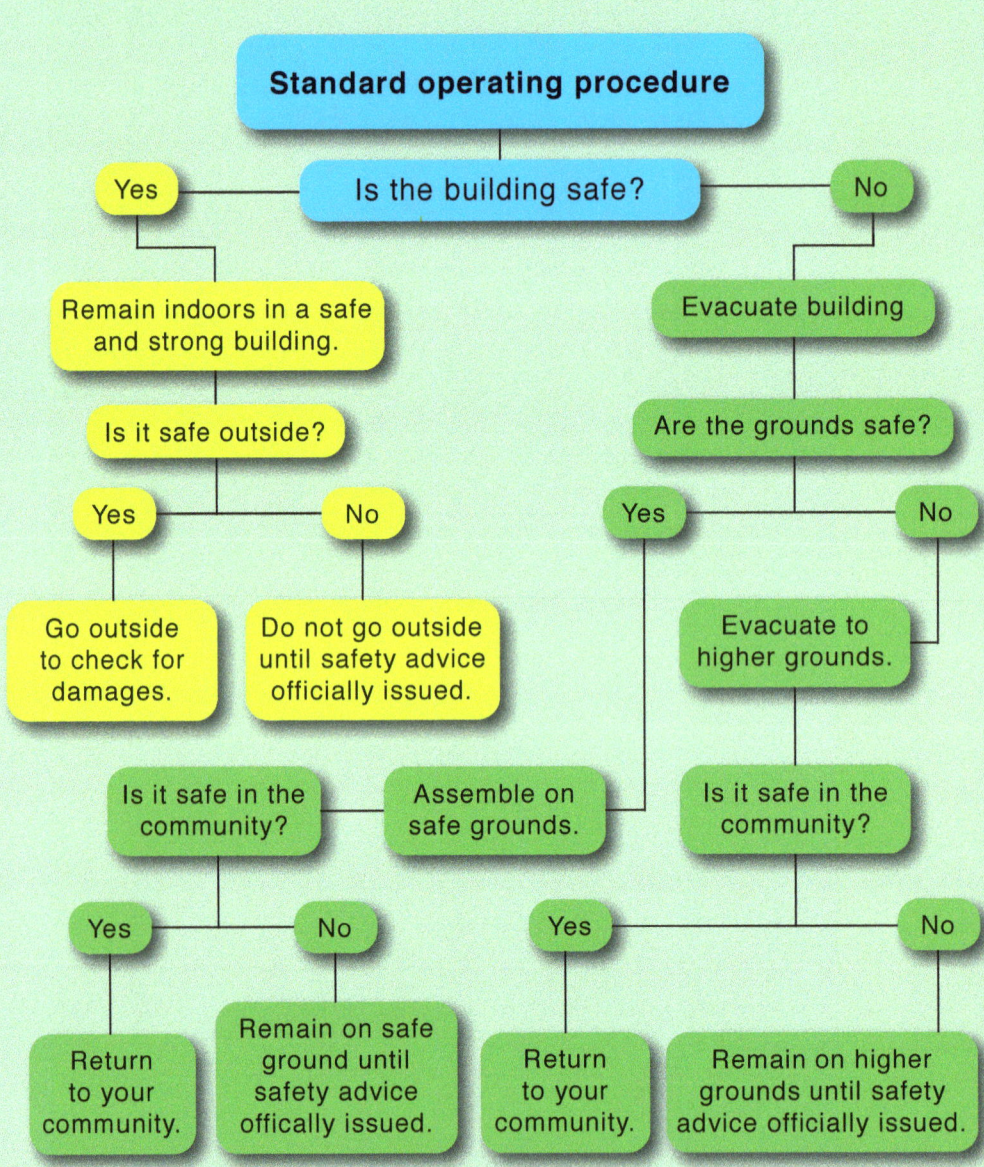

Supporting information

Emergency kit

Keep an emergency kit at home for your family.

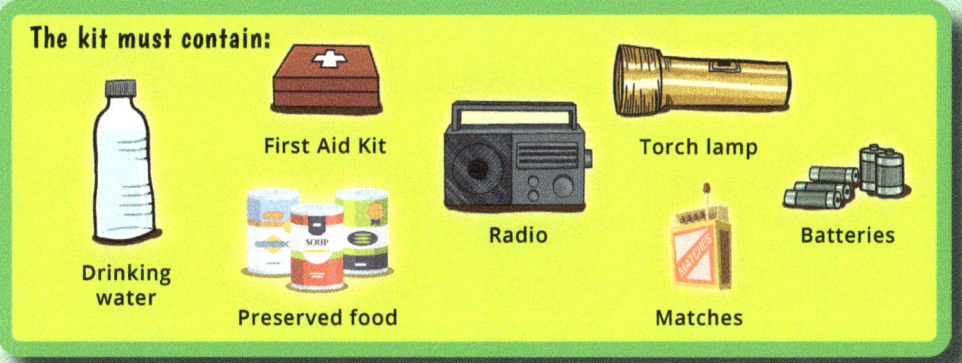

Use the kit only in case of emergency and replace anything that has been used.

Shelter-in-place

Earthquake:
- Identify safe places where you can protect your head and avoid heavy falling objects.
- Don't forget an earthquake can cause a tsunami.
- If you feel a strong earthquake, go quickly to higher ground, and listen to the radio for warnings.

Tropical cyclone:
- Open louvers on the side of the building, away from wind to reduce the pull force of the wind on the roof.
- Remain calm, stay indoors but clear of doors and windows.
- Remain in the strongest part of the building.

Do not go outside until safety advice is officially issued.

Evacuate building

Assist people with disability and visitors.
Take your emergency kit.
Evacuate to higher ground and move to a safe location.

Tsunami:
- Run to a safe place in high ground or at least 2 km inside the island.
- Wait for at least 2-3 hours after the first wave to return to the village.

Listen to the radio for further information or reach out to the emergency contacts.

You can use these questions to talk about this book with your family, friends and teachers.

What did you learn from this book?

Describe this book in one word. Funny? Scary? Colourful? Interesting?

How did this book make you feel when you finished reading it?

What was your favourite part of this book?

download our reader app
getlibraryforall.org

About the contributors

Library For All works with authors and illustrators from around the world to develop diverse, relevant, high quality stories for young readers. Visit libraryforall.org for the latest news on writers' workshop events, submission guidelines and other creative opportunities.

Did you enjoy this book?

We have hundreds more expertly curated original stories to choose from.

We work in partnership with authors, educators, cultural advisors, governments and NGOs to bring the joy of reading to children everywhere.

Did you know?

We create global impact in these fields by embracing the United Nations Sustainable Development Goals.

libraryforall.org

www.ingramcontent.com/pod-product-compliance
Lightning Source LLC
Chambersburg PA
CBHW040315050426
42452CB00018B/2860